MAHARASHTRA AS A LINGUISTIC PROVINCE

B. R. AMBEDKAR

TRUE SIGN
PUBLISHING HOUSE

Published by True Sign Publishing House
Address: 21, 2nd Floor, Kundan Nagar, Bagmugaliya,
Bhopal, Madhya Pradesh - 462026
E-mail: truesignbooks@gmail.com
Website: www.truesign.in

Maharashtra As A Linguistic Province

Author: B. R. Ambedkar

ISBN: 978-93-5988-540-7

First Edition: 2023

CONTENTS

NOTE

The figures quoted in this memorandum have been taken from various books and pamphlets written by various writers on the subject of reconstituting Maharashtra on a linguistic basis. I rely upon the writers for their accuracy. Similarly, the map of Maharashtra attached to this Memorandum need not be taken as accurate or complete. The idea is merely to give a picture of how the Province when reconstituted will look like.

B. R. Ambedkar.

14-10-48

PART - I

THE PROBLEM OF
LINGUISTIC PROVINCES

1.The question of Linguistic Provinces has not only led to a great deal of controversy born out of party prejudices and party interests but it has led to a difference of opinion as to the merits thereof. The points of controversy relate to claims and counter-claims as between contiguous Provinces to territories as well as to the terms of their inclusion. I shall deal with them at a later stage in so far as they relate to the creation of the

Maharashtra Province. I shall first take up the question of the merits of the proposal for Linguistic Provinces.

Purposes behind the demand for Linguistic Provinces

2. What is the purpose which lies behind the demand for Linguistic Provinces? The generality of those who advocate the creation of Linguistic Provinces do so because they believe that the Provinces have different languages and cultures. They should therefore have the fullest scope to develop their languages and their cultures. In other words, the Provinces have all the elements of a distinct nationality and they should be allowed the freedom to grow to their fullest in nationhood.

Difficulties arising out of Linguistic Provinces

3. In discussing the question of creating such Linguistic Provinces it would be very short-sighted to omit from one's consideration the fact that the structure of Government of India of the future is to be cast in

a dual form: (a) a Central Government and (b) a number of Provincial Governments inextricably inter-linked and inter-woven in the discharge of their respective Legislative, Executive and Administrative functions. Before one could agree to the creation of Linguistic Provinces, one must, therefore, consider the effects which Linguistic Provinces would have on the working of the Central Government.

4. Among the many effects that may be envisaged, the following are obvious:

1. Linguistic Provinces will result in creating as many nations as there are groups with pride in their race, language arid literature. The Central Legislature will be a League of Nations and the Central Executive may become a meeting of separate and solidified nations filled with the consciousness of their being separate in culture and therefore in interests. They may develop the mentality of political insubordination, i.e., refusal to obey the majority or of staging walk-outs. The development of such a mentality is not to be altogether discounted. If such a mentality grows it may easily make the working of the Central Government impossible.

2. The creation of Linguistic Provinces would be fatal to the maintenance of the necessary administrative relations between the Centre and the Provinces. If each Province adopts its own language as its official language the Central Government will have to correspond in as many official languages as there are Linguistic Provinces. This must be accepted as an impossible task. How great a deadlock Linguistic Provinces will create in the working of the Governmental machine can be better understood by studying the effects of Linguistic Provinces on the Judiciary. In the new set-up, each Province will have a High Court with a series of subordinate courts below it. At the apex of these High Courts will be the Supreme Court with the right to hear appeals against the decisions of the High Courts. On the basis of Linguistic Provinces, Courts of each Province including its High Court will conduct their proceedings in the language of the Province. What is the Supreme Court to do when its jurisdiction is invoked for rectifying a wrong done by the High Court ? The Supreme Court will have to close down. For, if it is to function — every judge of the Supreme Court — I am omitting for the moment (he lawyers practising therein — must know the language of every Province—which it is impossible to provide for.

No one can contemplate such a situation with equanimity. It may lead to a break-up of India. Instead of remaining united, India may end in becoming Europe — faced with the prospect of chaos and disorder.

Advantages from Linguistic Provinces

5. While it is true that the proposal of Linguistic Provinces creates a problem which goes to the very root of the matter — inasmuch as it affects the unity of India—there can be no doubt that the reconstruction of Provinces on linguistic basis has certain definite political advantages.

6. The main advantage of the scheme of Linguistic Provinces which appeals to me quite strongly is that Linguistic Provinces would make democracy work better than it would in mixed Provinces. A Linguistic Province produces what democracy needs, namely, social homogeneity. Now the homogeneity of a people depends upon their having a belief in a common origin, in the possession of a common language and literature, in their pride in a common historic tradition, community of social customs, etc. is a proposition which no student of sociology can dispute. The absence of a social homogeneity in a State creates a dangerous situation especially where such a State is raised on a democratic structure. History shows that democracy cannot work in a State where the population is not homogeneous. In a heterogeneous population divided into groups which are hostile and antisocial towards one another the working of democracy is bound to give rise to cases of discrimination, neglect, partiality, suppression of the interests of one group at the hands of another group which happens to capture political power. The reason why in an heterogeneous society, democracy cannot succeed is because power instead of being used impartially and on merits and for the benefit of all is used for the aggrandisement of one group and to the detriment of another. On the other hand, a state which is homogeneous in its population can work for the true ends of democracy, for there are no artificial barriers or social antipathies which lead to the misuse of political power.

7. It follows that if democracy is to function properly the subjects of the State must be so distributed as to form a single homogeneous group. The constitution for the Provinces of India which is on the anvil is designed for a democratic form of Government. It follows that each Province must be homogeneous in its population if democracy in the Province is to be successful. This is simply another way of saying that each Province must

be a linguistic unit if it is to be fitted to work a democratic constitution. Herein lies the justification for Linguistic Provinces.

Can the creation of Linguistic Provinces be postponed?

8. Can the solution of this problem be postponed ? In this connection, I would like to place before the Commission the following considerations :

i. There is nothing new in the demand for Linguistic Provinces. Six Provinces (1) East Punjab, (2) United Provinces, (3) Bihar, (4) West Bengal, (5) Assam and (6) Orissa already exist as Linguistic Provinces. The Provinces which are clamouring for being reconstituted on linguistic basis are: (1) Bombay, (2) Madras and (3) Central Provinces. When the principle of Linguistic Provinces is accepted in the case of six Provinces, the other Provinces which are asking the same principle to be applied to them, cannot be asked to wait indefinitely:

ii. The situation in the Non-Linguistic Provinces has become exasperating if not dangerous and is in no way different from the situation as it existed in the old Turkish Empire or in the old Austro-Hungarian Empire.

iii. The demand for Linguistic Provinces is an explosive force of the same character which was responsible for blowing up the old Turkish Empire or Austro-Hungarian Empire. It is better not to allow it to get too hot when it may become difficult to prevent an explosion.

iv. So long as the Provinces were not democratic in their constitutions and so long as they did not possess the widest sovereign powers which the new constitution gives them the urgency of Linguistic Provinces was not very great. But with the new constitution, the problem has become very urgent.

The solution of the difficulties

9. If the problem must be dealt with immediately what is to be the solution ? As has already been pointed out, the solution must satisfy two conditions. While accepting the principle of Linguistic Provinces it must provide against the break-up of India's unity. My solution of the problem therefore is that, while accepting the demand for the re-constitution of Provinces on linguistic basis, the constitution should provide that the official language of every Province shall be the same as the official language

of the Central Government. It is only on that footing that I am prepared to accept the demand for Linguistic Provinces.

10. l am aware of the fact that my suggestion runs counter to the conception of Linguistic Provinces which is in vogue. It is that the language of the Province shall be its official language. I have no objection to Linguistic Provinces. But I have the strongest objection to the language of the Province being made its official language where it happens to be different from the official language of the Centre. My objection is based on the following considerations:

1. The idea of having a Linguistic Province has nothing to do with the question of what should be its official language. By a Linguistic Province, I mean a Province which by the social composition of its population is homogeneous and therefore more suited for the realisation of those social ends which a democratic Government must fulfil. In my view, a Linguistic Province has nothing to do with the language of the Province. In the scheme of Linguistic Provinces, language has necessarily to play its part. But its part can be limited to the creation of the Province, i.e., for demarcation of the boundaries of the Province. There is no categorical imperative in the scheme of Linguistic Provinces which compels us to make the language of the Province its official language. Nor is it necessary, for sustaining the cultural unity of the Province, to make the language of the Province its official language. For, the cultural unity of the Province, which already exists, is capable of being sustained by factors other than language such as common historic tradition, community of social customs, etc. To sustain Provincial cultural unity which already exists it does not require the use of the Provincial language for official purposes. Fortunately for the Provincialists there is no fear of a Maharashtrian not remaining a Maharashtrian because he spoke any other language. So also there is no fear of a Tamilian or an Andhra or a Bengali ceasing to be a Tamilian, Andhra or Bengali if he spoke any other language than his own mother-tongue.

2. The out-and-out advocates of Linguistic Provinces would no doubt protest that they have no intention of converting the Provinces into separate nations. Their bona fides need not be doubted. At the same time, it often happens that things do take a shape which their authors never intended. It is therefore absolutely necessary to take from the very beginning every step to prevent things taking an evil

shape in course of time. There is therefore nothing wrong if the loosening of the ties in one direction is accompanied by their being tightened up in another direction.

3. We must not allow the Provincial language to become its official language eve" if it was natural that the Provincial language should be the official language of the Province. There is no danger in creating Linguistic Provinces. Danger lies in creating Linguistic Provinces with the language of each Province as its official language. The latter would lead to the creation of Provincial nationalities. For the use of the Provincial languages as official languages would lead Provincial cultures to be isolated crystallised, hardened and solidified. It would be fatal to allow this to happen. To allow this is to allow the Provinces to become independent nations, separate in everything and thus open the road to the ruination of United India. In Linguistic Provinces without the language of the Province being made its official language the Provincial culture would remain fluid with a channel open for give and take. Under no circumstances, we must allow the Linguistic Provinces to make their Provincial languages their official languages.

11. The imposition of an All-India official language on a Linguistic Province which may happen to be different from the language of the Province cannot come in the way of maintaining Provincial culture. Official language will be used only in the field occupied by Government. The nonofficial field or what may be the purely cultural field will still remain open to the Provincial language to play its part. There may be a healthy competition between the official and non-official language. One may try to oust the other. If the official language succeeds in ousting the non-official language from the cultural field, nothing like it. If it fails, there cannot be much harm. Such a position cannot be said to be intolerable. It is no more intolerable than the present position in which we have English as the official language and the Provincial language as its non-official language. The only difference is that the official language will not be English but some other.

The requirements of a satisfactory solution

12. I am aware of the fact that my solution is not an ideal solution. It makes working of the constitution in the Provinces on democratic lines possible. But it does not make possible the democratic working of the

constitution at the Centre. That is because mere linguistic unity, i.e., the facility to speak a common language does not ensure homogeneity which is the result of many other factors. As stated before, the representatives selected by the Provinces to the Central Legislature will remain what they are, namely, Bengalis, Tamilians, Andhras, Maharashtrians, etc., even though they may be speaking the official language of the Centre and not their mother- tongue. But an ideal solution which can be put into effect immediately, I cannot see. We must be content with the next best. The only thing we must be sure about is that the solution we adopt immediately must satisfy two conditions:

(i) It must be the very next best to the ideal; and (ii) It must be capable of developing itself into the ideal.

Judged in the light of these considerations, I venture to say that the solution which I have suggested satisfies these two conditions.

PART - II

WILL MAHARASHTRA BE A VIABLE PROVINCE ?

Tests of Viability

13. Coming to the specific question of Maharashtra Province it is necessary to be satisfied that it will be a viable Province. For being declared a viable Province, a Province must satisfy certain tests. It must be of a certain size, it must have a certain volume of population and a commensurate amount of revenue. A Province must not only be self-supporting—which any Province can be by choosing to live on a lower plane—but it must have sufficient revenue to provide for a minimum standard of administration required by efficiency and the needs of social welfare. Is **Maharashtra Viable?**

14. Does the Province of Maharashtra satisfy these tests? The following are the figures which show the size and population of the Maharashtra Province as constituted on a linguistic basis :

Territory   Area in square miles   Total Population of the territory Total Marathi speaking population of the territory   Percentage   of Marathi speaking population to total population

Territory	Area in square miles	Total Population of the territory	Total Marathi speaking population of the territory	Percentage of Marathi speaking population to total population
Twelve districts of the Bombay Presidency	47284	12913544	10045100	77.8
Eight Districts of and Berar C.P.	36865	7020694	5388300	76.7
Total	84151	19934238	15433400	77.4
States within Bombay Presidency	11314	2720207	2120700	77.9
Marathi speaking Districts of Hyderabad State	22766	4249272	3299300	77.6
Goa	1534	580000	520000	89.6
State of Bastar	13701	633888	212300	33.5
Total	49315	8183367	6142300	—
GRAND TOTAL	33466	28117605	21585700	76.8

Area and population of Maharashtra

15. The above table gives figures for the Maharashtra Province in its two forms (1) abridged and (2) unabridged. In its unabridged form which means if all the area occupied by the Marathi-speaking people was constituted in one single Province the area and the population of Maharashtra will be 1,33,466 square miles with a population of 2,15,85,700. In its abridged form which means that if the area and population of the Marathi- speaking people comprised within the States was for the moment omitted, even then the proposed Maharashtra Province would comprise an area of 84,151 square miles with a population of 1,54,33,400.

Revenue of Maharashtra

16. Turning to the revenue side of the Province, it has been estimated that the total annual revenue at the existing rate of taxation which will accrue to the abridged Maharashtra Province will be approximately Rs. 25,61,51.000.

Comparison of Maharashtra with other Provinces

17. Some comparisons are necessary to get an idea if a Province of this size, with this population and with so much revenue will be viable. For this, I give below figures of the first or the biggest and the forty-seventh or the smallest states within the U.S.A. in order of their size and population :

States	Area in Square Miles
1st Texas	2,67,339
47th Delaware	2,057
States	Population
1st New York	1,26,32,890
47th Wyoming	2,57,108

18. It is obvious that Maharashtra whether one takes its abridged edition or the unabridged edition of it will be several times bigger than Delaware which is the smallest State in U.S.A. in point of area and also several times bigger than New York which is the biggest state in U.S.A. in point of population.

19. Comparison of Maharashtra with the existing and prospective Linguistic Provinces of India may also be useful. Their position in point of area, population and revenue is as follows :

Province	Area in square miles	Population	Annual Revenue
Existing Linguistic Province -			
United Provinces	106247	55020617	326508000
Bihar	69745	36340151	162678000
Orissa	32198	8228544	46062000
New Linguistic Province-			
Andhra	70000	19000000	—
Karnatak	25000	4500000	—
Kerala	6000	3500000	---

These figures when compared with the figures for Maharashtra leave no doubt that Maharashtra will not merely be a viable Province but a strong province in point of area, population and revenue.

PART - III

SHOULD THE MAHARASHTRA PROVINCE BE FEDERAL OR UNITARY?

20. I will now turn to what are known to be points on which there is controversy. There is no controversy regarding the unification of Maharashtra into one Province. The controversy relates to the way it should he brought about. One view is that the new Maharashtra Province should be a unitary Province, with a single legislature and a single executive. The other view is that Maharashtra should be a Federation of two sub-provinces, one sub-province to consist of the Marathi-speaking districts of the Bombay Presidency and the other of the Marathi-speaking districts of the present Province of the Central Provinces and Berar. The idea of creating sub-Provinces has originated from the spokesmen of the Marathi-speaking districts of Central Provinces and Berar. I am satisfied that it is only the wish of a few high-caste politicians who feel that in a unified Maharashtra their political careers will come to an end. It has no backing from the people of e fact that it gives me an opportunity to enunciate what I regard as a very vital principal. When it is decided to create a Linguistic Province, I am definitely of opinion that all areas which are contiguous and which speak the same language should be forced to come into it. There should be no room for choice nor for self-determination. Every attempt must be made to create larger provincial units. Smaller provincial units will be a perpetual burden in normal times and a source of weakness in an emergency. Such a situation must be avoided. That is why I insist that all parts of Maharashtra should be merged together in a single province.

PART - IV

MAHARASHTRA AND THE CITY OF BOMBAY

Controversy over Bombay

21. Should the City of Bombay be included in Maharashtra or not is another point over which there has been a controversy. A meeting was held in Bombay in the building of the Indian Merchants Chamber. The meeting was attended by no more than sixty. With the exception of one Indian-Christian it was attended by only Gujarati- speaking merchants and industrialists. Although it was small and sectional meeting, its proceedings were flashed on the front page of every important newspaper in India and the Times of India was so impressed by its importance that it wrote an editorial which while mildly castigating the vituperative tone which the speakers at the meeting adopted against the Maharashtrians, supported the resolutions passed at the meeting regarding the future of Bombay. This proves what truth there is in the reply given by Lord Birkenhead to the Irish Leader, Mr. Redmond, in the course of the Irish controversy when he said that there are cases where a minority is a majority.

My memorandum would be woefully incomplete if I omitted to deal with the pros and cons of this controversy. This is because of two reasons: In the first place, the meeting has been recognized to be very important and secondly because the resolutions of the meeting have been supported by eminent University Professors.

Proposals regarding Bombay

22. The meeting passed the following resolutions:

1. That the question of the creation of Linguistic Provinces should be postponed; or

2. That if it is not postponed, Bombay City should be constituted into a separate Province.

There is a third suggestion, namely, that Konkan should be constituted into a separate Province with Bombay as its capital. There is hardly any support to this plan. There is therefore no necessity to discuss it.

Decision regarding Bombay must be made now

23. I have no complaint against that part of the Resolution which says the question of Linguistic Provinces be postponed provided the main question namely whether Bombay should or should not be included in Maharashtra is settled. If this question was settled it did not matter if it took five or ten years to give effect to the Settlement. But the resolution is only an escapism. It does not settle the issue. It only adjourns the controversy. The main question must therefore be tackled right now.

Ground for the exclusion of Bombay from Maharashtra

24. The arguments urged in favour of separating Bombay from Maharashtra are set out below :

1. Bombay was never a part of Maharashtra*.

2. Bombay was never a part of the Maratha Empire.

3. The Marathi-speaking people do not form a majority of the population of the City of Bombay.

4. Gujarathis have been old residents of Bombay.

5. Bombay is a trade centre for vast areas outside Maharashtra. Therefore, Bombay cannot be claimed by Maharashtra. It belongs to the whole of India.

6. It is the Gujarathi speaking people of Bombay who have built up the trade and industry of Bombay. The Maharashtrians have been only clerks and coolies. It would be wrong to place the owners of trade and industry under the political dominance of the working classes who form the bulk of Maharashtrians.

7. Maharashtra wants Bombay to be included in Maharashtra because it wants to live on the surplus of Bombay

8. A multi-lingual State is better. It is not so fatal to the liberty of smaller people.

9. Regrouping of Provinces should be on rational lines and not on national lines.

Burden of Proof

25. On an examination of these paints it is obvious that points (1) and (2) are preliminary in the sense that they help us to decide on whom rests the burden of proof. If it is proved that Bombay is part of Maharashtra, then the burden of proof for separating it from Maharashtra must tall upon those who urge that it should be separated and not upon those who claim that it should remain part of Maharashtra. I will therefore deal with these two points first.

POINTS (1) and (2) Verdict of History

26. These points can be considered both in the light of history as well as of geography. I am, however, convinced that history cannot help us to decide the issue. In the first place, how far back must we go to find the data on which to base our conclusion. It is obvious that the history of the ancient past would be of no use to us in this connection. What could be of use to us is the past of the present. One may go further and question any reliance being placed upon such a past of the present for drawing any conclusion that can have a bearing on the issue before us. Most of the contacts between people during historical times have been between conquerors and conquered. This is true of India as well as of Europe. But the results of such contacts have been quite different in Europe and in India. In Europe such contacts have produced assimilation of the conflicting social elements. Frequent inter-marriages have confounded the original stocks. One language, either the most useful or the most commonly spoken, has tended to supplant the other. If one civilisation is superior to the others in the same country it has automatically supplanted them. This natural tendency towards assimilation which we see in Europe is so strong that steps have to be taken to counteract it. What is the tendency in India ? It is definitely against assimilation. The Musalmans conquered Hindus. But the Musalmans remained Musalmans and the Hindus remained Hindus. The Gujarathis were conquered by Maharashtrians and were ruled by them

for some years. What effect has it produced upon the Gujarathis ? Nothing. Gujarathis have remained Gujarathis and Maharashtrians have remained Maharashtrians. The Chalukyas conquered Maharashtrians and so did the Shilahars. But there was no assimilation between them. The Shilahars and Chalukyas remained what they were and so did the Maharashtrians. This being the case, what help can Indian History give in the decision of the issue? The history of internal upheavals as well as of external aggressions has been nothing more than a passing show. Conquest means nothing and proves nothing.

Verdict of Geography

27. Let us now turn to geography and ask for its verdict. It seems to be & better witness than history. For this purpose one must consider the location of Bombay in relation to the Province of Maharashtra. The Province of Maharashtra once it is created will be triangular in shape. One side of this triangle is formed by the Western Coast Line of India between Daman in the North and Karwar in the South. The City of Bombay lies in between Daman and Karwar. The Province of Gujarat starts from Daman and spreads northwards. The Kanada Province starts from Karwar and spreads southwards. It is about 85 miles South of Daman which is the starting point of Gujarat, and 250 miles North of Karwar, which is the starting point of Karnatak Province. If the unbroken territory between Daman and Karwar is geographically part of Maharashtra, how could Bombay be held not to be a part of Maharashtra ? This is an incontrovertible fact of nature. Geography has made Bombay part of Maharashtra. Let those who want to challenge the fact of nature do so. To an unbiased mind it is conclusive proof that Bombay belongs to Maharashtra.

Bombay and the Maratha Empire

28. That the Marathas did not care to make it a part of their Empire does in no way affect the validity of the conclusion drawn from geography. That the Marathas did not care to conquer it does not prove that Bombay is not a part of Maharashtra. It only means that the Maratha power was a land power and did not therefore care to spend its energy in the conquest of a seaport.

29. With the decision on Points (1) and (2), the burden must now shift

on those who contended that Bombay should not be included in Maharashtra. Have they discharged the burden ? This leads to the consideration of other points.

         Maharashtra As A Linguistic Province

POINT (3)

Marathi-speaking population—majority or minority

30. There is no unanimity on this question. Prof. Gadgil speaking for the inclusion of Bombay in Maharashtra asserts that the Marathi-speaking population of Bombay according to the census of 1941 is 51 per cent. Speaking against the inclusion of Bombay, Prof. Gheewala says that the Marathi-speaking population of Bombay is 41 percent Prof. Vakil has brought it down to 39 percent which he regards as a very liberal estimate. I have not had time to check up these figures and I understand that the Census of Bombay does not render much help in arriving at a precise figure. However, if one reads the reasons assigned by Prof. Vakil, one would find his conclusion to be speculative it not wishful thinking. But assuming that5: the figures given by Prof. Vakil are correct, what of it ? What conclusion can be drawn from it ? Does it defeat the claim of Maharashtra to include Bombay ? Ever since the British became the masters of India, India has been one country with a right to free movement from place to place. If people from all parts of India were allowed to come to Bombay and settle there, why should the Maharashtrians suffer ? it is not their fault. The present state of the population cannot therefore be a ground for excluding Bombay from Maharashtra.

POINT (4)

Are Gujarathis Natives Of Bombay?

31. Let us however fully consider the question. Are the Gujarathis natives of Bombay ? If they are not, how did they come to Bombay ? What is the source of their wealth ? No Gujarathi would clam that the Gujarathis are the natives of Bombay. If they are not the natives of Bombay, how did they come to Bombay ? Like the Portuguese, the French, the Dutch and the English on adventures to fight their way through and willing to take any risks? The answers which history gives to these questions are quite clear. The Gujarathis did not come to Bombay voluntarily. They were brought to Bombay by the officers of the East India Company to serve as commercial Adatias or go-betweens. They were brought because the East India Company's officers who had their first factory in Surat had got used to Surti Banias as their go-betweens in carrying on their trade. This explains the entry of Gujarathis in Bombay. Secondly, the Gujarathis did not come to Bombay to trade on the basis of free and equal competition with other traders. They came as privileged persons with certain trading rights given

to them exclusively by the East India Company. Their importation into Bombay was considered for the first time in the year 1671 by Governor Aungier. This fact is referred to in the Gazetteer of Bombay Town and Island. Vol. I in the following terms :

"Another scheme for the advantage of. Bombay in which Governor Aungier interested himself was the settlement of Surat Banias in Bombay. It appears that the Mahajan or committee of the Surat Bania community desired the assurance of certain privileges before risking the move to Bombay and that the company had given a general approval to the Mahajan's proposal. On the 10th January the Surat Council wrote to the Company. The Mahajan or Chief Council of the Banias have been much satisfied with the answer which you were pleased to give to their petition sent you by the ship Samson touching their privileges in Bombay. It seems they have determined once more to trouble Your Honours with a letter which they have ordered your broker Bhimji Parakh to write, representing their desires that the said privileges may be confirmed to them under your great seal, for which their request they give you their reason and ground in their own letter which they have sent us to be transmitted to you and now goes in your packet by ship Falcon. The argument they use to strengthen their request seems to have some weight. They say the Honourable Company are perpetual and their ordinances always of force, but their Presidents and Councils are mutable, and the succeeding Presidents and Councils, do alter often what their predecessors have granted on which score they hope your Honours will be pleased to grant their petition. As to our judgments hereon, we humbly offer that we cannot see any detriment can accrue to you thereby, rather a considerable advantage may follow; and as to the latitude and extent of what privileges you shall afford them, it must be totally referred to your own wisdoms howsoever you shall please to determine in this matter. We judge if your Honours would please to favour them with a line in answer to their letter, it would be a great comfort to them and no disadvantage to your interest."

32. What were the privileges which the Gujrarathi Banias had asked for from the East India Company ? The following petition by one Nima Parakh, an eminent Bania belonging to the City of Diu, gives some idea of what they were:

"1. That the Honourable Company shall allot him so much ground in or near the present town free of rent as shall be judged necessary to build a house or warehouse thereon.

"2. That he with the Brahmans of Vers (Gors or priests) of his caste shall enjoy the free exercise of their religion within their own houses without the molestation of any person whatsoever; that no Englishman, Portuguese, or other Christian nor Muhammadan shall be permitted to live within their compound or offer to kill any living creature there, or do the least injury or indignity to them, and if any shall presume to offend them within the limits of their said compound, upon their complaint to the Governor (at Surat) or Deputy Governor (at Bombay), the offenders shall be exemplarily punished; that they shall have liberty to burn their dead according to their custom, also to use their ceremonies at their weddings ; and that none of their profession of what age, sex or condition whatever they be, shall be forced to turn Christians, nor to carry burthens against their wills.

"3. That he and his family shall be free from all duties of watch and ward, or any charge and duty depending thereon; that neither the Company nor the Governor, Deputy Governor or Council, or any other person, shall on any pretence whatsoever force them to lend money for public or private account or use any indirect.

"4. That in case there falls out any difference or suit in law between him or his vakil or attorneys or the Banias of his caste, and any other persons remaining on the island, the Governor or Deputy Governor shall not suffer him or them to be publicly arrested dishonoured or carried to prison, without first giving him due notice of the cause depending, that he or they may cause justice to be done in an honest and amicable way and in case any difference happen between him or his attorney and any Bania of their own caste, they may have liberty to decide it among themselves without being forced to go to law.

"5. That he shall have liberty of trade in his own ships and vessels to what port he pleases, and come in and go out when he thinks good; without paying anchorage, having first given the Governor or Deputy Governor or customer notice and taken their consent thereunto.

"6. That in case he brings any goods on shore more than he can sell on the island within the space of 12 months, he shall have liberty to transport them to what port he pleases, without paying custom for exportation.

"7. That in case any person be indebted to him, and also to other Banias, and be not able to pay all his debts, his right may be preferred before other Banias.

"8. That in case of war. or any other danger which may succeed, he shall have a warehouse in the castle to secure his goods, treasure, and family therein.

"9. That he or any of his family shall have liberty of egress and regress to and from the fort or residence of the Governor or Deputy Governor; that they shall be received with civil respect and be permitted to sit down according to their qualities; that they shall freely use coaches, horses or palanquins and quitasols (that is barsums or umbrellas) for their convenience without any disturbances ; that their servants may wear swords and daggers, shall not be abused, beaten or imprisoned except they offend, and that in case of any of his kindred or friends shall come to visit him or them from any other ports, they shall be used with civility and respect.

"10. That he and his assigns shall have liberty to sell and buy coconuts, betelnuts, pan or betel-leaves, and any other commodity not rented out without any molesiation on the island."

33. How this petition of Nima Parakh was disposed of can be seen from the reply of the Deputy Governor of Bombay dated 3rd April. 1677, which was in the following terms :

"According to order we have consider the articles of Nima Parakh Bania, which if we rightly understand we do not apprehend any prejudice connection the most of them being what the meanest enjoy.

"The first is very easy, the Company having vast ground enough, and we daily do the same to Banias and others who come to inhabit here. As to the second, the free exercise of religion is permitted to all with the use of their ceremonies at: weddings and feast, the Banias always burning their dead without molestation. Neither do we permit any person to kill anything near the Banias who ail live by themselves, much less can any person presume to enter into anybody's house or compound without the owner's license; and, for forcing people to turn Christian against their wills, the whole world will vindicate us; neither are any persons forced to carry burdens against their wills. No Bania, Brahman, Moor, or such man is obliged to watch or ward or other duty, but if any person buys an oart or warge (vada) he is bound on every alarm to send a musquiter. But if he possesses no land no duty is exacted, so the articles may be granted to Nima. and when he goes about to buy any land he may be acquainted with that small encumbrance thereon.

"The 4th article is indeed a privilege but no more than Girdhar, the Moody and some others have, which does not in the least exempt them from the hands of the law or justice, but does only ask that justice be done respectfully, which he need not doubt of... and for matter of differences among themselves there is already his Honour's patent authorising them to decide such things.

"As to the 5th, the great anchorage of a rupee per ton is wholly taken off. There remains only a small one of a rupee for every 100 tons, which is so inconsiderable a matter that we do not believe we will stick at it. If he does, it will amount but to a small matter being only for his own vessels that the Company may easily allow it.

"The 6th if we rightly apprehend it, is no more than what all people enjoy, who are so far from paying custom at exportation of their own goods that they pay none for what goods they buy. But if he intends his goods must pay no custom at landing nor none at exportation of what he cannot sell, it will be so great a loss to the Company, they having farmed out the customs for two years, that the benefit of his settling here, will, we believe, not countervail it, till it comes into the Company's hands again,

"As to the 7th, our law is such that if a person be indebted to several men, whosoever gets a judgment first in Court will be paid his full debt, but no man can be aggrieved at that, nor can any creditor have any pretence to what is once paid, and when judgment is given it is already paid in law, so that. he is no longer proprietor of it But when a person is indebted to two men and the first sues him and upon that the second comes in and sues him too, with what justice can we pay all the debtor's estate to the second creditor. Only of this he may be assured that all justice shall be done him with speed according to our law and the party forced to pay the full debts if able, and be in prison for the rest till he pleases to release him, which we suppose may well content him.

"As to the 8th in case of war all person of quality have liberty to repair to the castle and secure their money and other things of value. Nor that I suppose be intends to fill up the castle with gari (coarse) goods ; but for money, jewels household stuff ,cloth goods of value that take up small room he may bring what he pleases and may have a warehouse apart allotted for himself and family.

"The 9th and 10th we may join together, they being only to fill up the number. They are plain optics to show the nature of those they live under. which, when they have experimented our Government, themselves will laugh at us, enjoying more freedom than the very articles demand for the meanest person is never denied egress and regress upon respectful notice given and for horses and coaches and the like he may keep as many as he pleases and his servants be permitted to wear what arms they please, a thing common to all. Nothing is more promoted by us than the free liberty for buying and selling which is the load-stone of trade.

"That last thing he asked of having 10 mans of tobacco free of all duties is the most difficult thing of all, for the farmers will ask a vast deal to grant such a licence/it being a very great profit they make in the sale of 10 mans, so that we know not which way this article can be condescended to, but in this your Honours can judge better than us."

34. In reply on the 26th April, the Surat Council wrote : " We observe your answer touching the articles proposed by Nima Parakh Bania in order to his settlement on Bombay. When we come again to treat with him thereon, we hope so to moderate the affair that the island shall not receive any the least prejudice thereby and we do not question but wholly to put him by his request to 10 mans of tobacco which he would annually receive or bring on the island free of all duties."

POINT (5)

Bombay—an Emporium of India

35. That Bombay is an emporium for the whole of India may be admitted. But it is difficult to understand how it can be said that because of this, Maharashtra cannot claim Bombay. Every port serves a much larger area than the country to which it belongs. No one, on that account, can say the country in which the port is situated cannot claim it as a part of its territory. Switzerland has no port. It uses either German, Italian or French Ports. Can the Swiss therefore deny the right of Germany, Italy or France, the territorial rights of their ports. Why then should Maharashtrians be denied the right to claim Bombay merely because it serves as a port for Provinces other than Maharashtra ? It would be different if the Province of Maharashtra were to get a right to close the Port to Non- Maharashtrians. Under the constitution, it will not have that right. Consequently, the inclusion of Bombay in Maharashtra will not affect the right of non-Maharashtrians to use the port as before.

POINT (6)

Gujarathis--owners of Trade and Industry of Bombay

36. It may be granted that the Gujarathis have a monopoly of trade. But, as has already been pointed out, this monopoly, they have been able to

establish because of the profits they were able to make which were the result of the privileges given to them by the East India Company on their settlement in Bombay. Who built up the trade and industry of Bombay is a matter for which no very great research is necessary. There is no foundation in fact for the statement that the trade and industry of Bombay was built up by Gujarathis. It was built up by Europeans and not by Gujarathis. Those who assert that it is the Gujarathis who did it should consult the Times of India Directory before making such a claim. The Gujarathis have been just merchants which is quite a different thing from being industrialists.

37. Once it is established that Bombay belonged to Maharashtra the claim of Maharashtra to include Bombay cannot be defeated by the argument that the trade and industry of Bombay is owned by the Gujarathis. The claim of mortgagor to his land cannot be defeated by the mortgagee on the ground that the mortgagee has built up permanent structures on the land. The Gujarathis assuming they have built up the trade and industry of Bombay are in no better position than a mortgagee is.

38. But who have built up the trade and industry of Bombay seems to me quite irrelevant to the decision of the issue whether Bombay should or should not be included in Maharashtra. This argument based on monopoly of trade and industry is really a political argument. It means that the owners may rule the workers but the workers must not be allowed to rule the owners. Those who use this argument do not seem to know what they are up against. The one thing they are up against is whether this argument is to be confined only to the City of Bombay or whether it is to have a general application.

39. There is no reason why it should not have a general application. For just as in Bombay City society is divided into owners and workers or into capitalists and wage-earners, such also is the case of society in Gujarat or for the matter of that in every province of India. If the owners and capitalists of Bombay are to be protected by the exclusion of Bombay from Maharashtra because Maharashtrians belong to the working classes, what is the method they suggest for protecting the capitalists of Gujarat from the working classes of Gujarat. Those Gujarathi Professors like Vakils and Dantwalas who are searching their brains to supply arguments to the Gujarathi capitalists of Bombay have not thought of finding ways and means for protecting the Gujarathi capitalists of Gujarat against the working classes of Gujarat. The only remedy they can suggest is the abandonment of adult suffrage. That is the only way by which they can

protect the capitalists if they are out to protect capitalists in general and not the Gujarathi capitalists of Bombay in particular.

40. There is however one argument which the Professors could urge. It is that the Maharashtrians being in a majority would discriminate against the Gujarathi capitalists of Bombay if Bombay was included in Maharashtra.

One could appreciate such an argument. But those who like to use this argument must remember two things :

i. That Maharashtra is not the only place in which such a situation can arise. It may arise in any province. I like to refer to Bihar. In Bihar the land in which coal is found belongs to the people of Bihar. But the coal-owners are Gujarathis, Kathiawaris or Europeans. Is there no possibility of Biharis making a discrimination against Gujarathi and Kathiawari coal-owners ? Are the coalfields of Bihar to be excluded from the Province of Bihar and constituted into a separate Province in the interest of Kathiawari and Gujarathi coal-owners ?

ii. The constitution of India has noted the possibility of discrimination being made against a minority and has made more than ample provision for preventing it. There the fundamental rights. There are the provisions against discrimination; there are the provisions of payment of compensation, and there are the High Courts with the inherent rights to issue high prerogative writs both against individuals and Governments to stop any harm, injustice or harassment being done to any citizen. What more protection do the Gujarathi traders and industrialists of Bombay want against the possibility of discrimination ?

POINT (7)

Maharashtra's eye on Bombay's surplus

41. Before accusing Maharsshtrians of having an eye on the surplus of Bombay it must be proved that Bombay has a surplus. What appears as surplus is due really to bad accounting. It is bad accounting where expenditure on overhead charges such as (1) the Governor and his establishment, (2) the Ministers and their establishments, (3) the Legislature and the expenditure thereon, (4) Judiciary, (5) Police and (6) Provincial establishments such as those of the Commissioners of Police and Directors of Public Instruction is not being taken into account. I doubt very much if on the existing basis of taxation, Bombay will have any surplus

if expenditure on these items is charged to Bombay. It is a fallacy to charge all such expenditure to Maharashtra and exempt Bombay from it and then argue that Bombay has a surplus.

42. The statement that the Maharashtrians want Bombay because they want to live on the surplus revenue of Bombay, besides being wrong in fact raises a question of motive. I do not know if the Maharashtrians are actuated by any such motive. They are not a commercial community. Unlike other communities, the Maharashtrians have no nose for money, and I am one of these who believe that it is one of their greatest virtues. Money has never been their god. It is no part of their culture. That is why they have allowed all other communities coming from outside Maharashtra to monopolize the trade and industry of Maharashtra. But as I have shown there is no surplus and no question of Maharashtrians casting their eyes on it.

43. But supposing such a motive in the minds of the Maharashtrians, what is wrong in it? It is quite open to Maharashtrians to contend that they have a greater claim on Bombay's surplus because they have played and they will continue to play a greater part in supplying labour for the building up of the trade and industry of Bombay more than the people from other Provinces have done or likely to do. It would be difficult for any economist with any reputation to save who could deny that labour has as much claim on the wealth produced as capital if not more.

44. Secondly, the surplus from Bombay is not consumed by Maharashtra alone but is consumed by the whole of India. The proceeds of the Income-tax, Super-tax, etc. which Bombay pays to the Central Government are all spent by the Central Government for all-India purposes and is shared by all other Provinces. To Prof. Vakil it does not matter if the surplus of Bombay is eaten up by United Provinces, Bihar, Assam, Orissa, West Bengal, East Punjab and Madras. What he objects to is Maharashtra getting any part of it. This is not an argument. It is only an exhibition of his hatred for Maharashtrians.

45. Granting that, Bombay was made into a separate Province, what I don't understand is how Prof. Vakil is going to prevent Maharashtra from getting share of Bombay surplus revenue. Even if Bombay is made separate

Province, Bombay will have to pay income-tax, super-tax, etc. and surely Maharashtra will get a part of the revenue paid by Bombay to the Centre either directly or indirectly. As I have said the argument has in it more malice than substance.

POINTS (8) AND (9)

General arguments against the inclusion of Bombay in Maharashtra

46. I will now turn to the Points (8) and (9) which have been urged by Professors Dantwala and Gheewala. Their arguments strike at the very root of the principle of Linguistic Provinces. As such I should have dealt with them in Part I of this Memorandum. But as the aim of their argument is to exclude Bombay from being included in Maharashtra, I have thought it proper to deal with them in this Part of the Memorandum as they are really arguments against the inclusion of Bombay in Maharashtra.

47. The sum total of the arguments of the two Professors is that Linguistic Provinces are bad. This cry against Linguistic Provinces is too late. Since when two Professors having been holding these views is not known. Are they opposed to Gujarat being reconstituted on Linguistic Provinces also has not been made clear by them. Or, is it that they believed in the principle of Linguistic Provinces but hurried to disavow it when they realized that the admission of the principle involves the surrender of Bombay to Maharashtra. It is perhaps one of these cases where a person not finding argument limited to his purpose is forced to resort to an argument which proves more than he is anxious to allow. I am, however, prepared to examine the substance of their argument.

48. Prof. Dantwala relies upon Lord Acton and quotes the following passage from his Essay on Nationality printed in his well-known book The History of Freedom and Other Essays in support of his own view against Linguistic Provinces. The quotation reads as follows :

"The combination of various nations in one State is a necessary condition of civilized life as the combination of men in society."

49. I am sorry to say that this quotation completely misrepresents Lord Acton. The quotation is only a few opening lines of a big passage. The full passage reads as follows :

"The combination of different nations in one State is as necessary a condition of civilized life as the combination of men in society. Inferior races are raised by living in political union with races intellectually superior. Exhausting and decaying nations are revived by the contact of younger vitality. Nations in which the elements of organization and the capacity for Government have been lost, either through the demoralizing influence of despotism or the disintegrating action of democracy, are restored and educated anew under the discipline of a stronger and less corrupted race. This fertilizing and regenerating process can only be obtained by living under one Government. It is in the cauldron of the State that the fusion takes place by which the vigour, the knowledge and the capacity of one portion of mankind may be communicated to another.

50. Why Prof. Dantwala left out the rest of the passage, it is difficult to understand. I am not suggesting that it is a deliberate case of suppresio veri and suggestio falsi. The fact is that it does misrepresent Lord Acton. Why has the Professor relied upon this passage, I do not understand. It is quite obvious that if the inferior races are placed in common with the superior races, the inferior races may improve. But the question is, who is inferior or who is superior. Are the Gujarathis inferior to Maharashtrians ? Or are the Maharashtrians inferior to Gujarathis ? Secondly, what is the channel of communion between Gujarathis and Maharashtrians which can assure the fusion of the two ? Prof. Dantwala has not considered the question. He found a sentence in Lord Acton's Essay and jumped at it for he could find nothing else to support his case. The point is that there is nothing in the message which has any relevance to the principle involved in the question of Linguistic Province.

51. So much for Prof. Dantwala's arguments. I will now examine Prof. Gheewala's arguments. Prof. Gheewala also relies on Lord Acton. He quotes a portion of a passage from Lord Acton's Essay on Nationality. I reproduce below the passage in full :

"The greatest adversary of the rights of nationality is the modern theory of nationality. By making the State and the nation commensurate with each other in theory, it reduces practically to a subject condition all other nationalities that may be within the boundary. It cannot admit them to an equality with the ruling nation which constitutes the State, because the State would then cease to be national, which would be a contradiction of the principle of its existence. According, therefore, to the degree of humanity and civilization in that dominant body which claims all the rights of the community, the inferior races are exterminated, or reduced to servitude, or outlawed, or put in a condition of dependence."

52. I do riot understand why the learned Professor has dragged in the name of Lord Acton. The passage does not really help him. There is one thing which seems to be uppermost in his mind. He thinks that if Bombay is included in Maharashtra the Province of Maharashtra will consist of two nationalities —one consisting of the Marathi-speaking people and the

other of the Gujarathi-speaking people and the Marathi-speaking people who would be the dominant class will reduce the Gujarathi-speaking people to a subject condition. It is in support of this he thought of citing Lord Acton. Such a possibility is always there. There is no objection to the way in which he has presented the problem. But there are great objections to the conclusions he draws.

53. In the first place, in a country like India in which society is throughout communally organized it is obvious that in whatever way it is divided into areas for administrative purposes, in every area there will always be one community which by its numbers happens to be a dominant community. As a dominant community it becomes a sole heir to all political power, which the area gets. If Marathi-speaking people in a unified Maharashtra with Bombay thrown into it will become dominant over the Gujarathi-speaking people, will this prospect be confined to Maharashtra only ? Will such a phenomena not occur within the Marathi-speaking people ? Will it not be found in Gujarat if Gujarat became a separate Province ? I am quite certain that within the Marathi-speaking people who are sharply divided between the Marathas and the non-Marathas, the Marathas being a dominant class will reduce both Gujarathi-speaking and the non-Marathas to a subject condition. In the same way in Gujarat in some parts the Anavil Brahmins from a dominant class. In other parts it is the Patidars who form a dominant class. It is quite likely that the Anavils and the Patidars will reduce the condition of the other communities to subjection. The problem therefore is not a problem peculiar to Maharashtra. It is a general problem.

54. What is the remedy for this problem ? Prof. Gheewala believes that the remedy lies in having a mixed State. So far as this remedy is concerned it is not his own. He has adopted it from Lord Acton. But I have no doubt that so far as Lord Acton advocates this remedy he is quite wrong. Lord Acton cites the case of Austria in support of his view. Unfortunately, Lord Acton did not live to see the fate of Austria. It was a mixed State. But far from providing for the safety of nationalities the clash of nationalities blew up Austria to bits. The real remedy is not a mixed State but an absolute State with no power to the people which is generally captured by a communal majority and exercised in the name of the people. Is Prof. Gheewala prepared for this remedy ? One need have no doubt to what his answer would be.

55. In the second place. Prof. Gheewala has confounded nationality in the social sense of the term with Nationality in its legal and political sense.

People often speak of nationality in speaking about Linguistic Provinces. Such use of the term can be only in the non-legal and non-political sense of the term. In my scheme there is no room even for the growth of separate provincial nationality. My proposal nips it in the bud. But even if the commonly suggested pattern of Linguistic Provinces with the language of the Province as the official language were adopted. Provinces cannot have that attribute of sovereignty which independent nations have.

56. It is very difficult to understand what exactly what Prof. Gheewala wants. Broadly he wants two things : He wants a mixed State and he also wants that a dominant section should not be in a position to reduce the smaller sections to subjection. I cannot see how Linguistic Provinces can come in the way of achieving it. For even after Provinces have been re-constituted on linguistic basis,—

1. Provinces will continue to be a conglomeration of communities which will give Prof. Gheewala the mixed State that he wants;

2. If Prof. Gheewala wants a more pronounced form of a mixed State to protect smaller communities or nationalities, he will certainly have it at the Centre.

As I have said, I do not think a mixed State is either a good State or stable State. But if Prof. Gheewala prefers it, he will have it in one form or another, both in the Provinces as well as at the Centre, in the former in the form of different communities and in the latter in the form of the representatives of different Provinces.

57. With regard to his second objective, there will be double protection. In the first place, the citizen will have such protection as a mixed State he thinks can give. Secondly, citizenship will be common throughout India.

There is no provincial citizenship. A Gujarathi in Maharashtra will have the same rights of citizenship in Maharashtra as Maharashtrian will have.

Given these facts, I fail to understand what objection Prof. Gheewala can have to Linguistic Provinces ?

58. Prof. Gheewala has made two other recommendations. He says, (1) if Provinces have to be reconstituted, constitute them on rational basis rather than on linguistic basis and (2) make nationality a personal thing.

59. To reconstitute Provinces on economic basis—which is what is meant by rational basis—appears more scientific than reconstituting them on linguistic basis. However, unscientific linguistic reorganization of

Provinces I cannot see how they can come in the way of rational utilization of economic resources of ndia. Provincial boundaries are only administrative boundaries. They do not raise economic barriers for the proper utilization of economic resources. If the position was that the resources contained within a Linguistic Province must only be explained by the people of the Province and no other than it could no doubt be said that the scheme of Linguistic Provinces was mischievous. But such is not the case. So long as Linguistic Provinces are not allowed to put a ban on the exploitation of the resources of the people by any body capably of wishing to exploit them a Linguistic Province will yield all the advantages of a rationally planned Province.

60. The proposal of making nationality as a personal thing and put it on the same footing as religion may be dismissed as being to Utopian. It would raise many administrative problems. It will come when the world is one and all nationals are its citizens. Nationality will automatically vanish as being quite useless.

61. So far I have dealt with the arguments advanced by those who are opposed to the inclusion of Bombay in Maharashtra. I have taken pains to do so not because I felt that they were very weighty. I did so because I felt it desirable to prevent the common man from being misled. The possibility of this happening was there and for two reasons. In the first place, those who have come forward with these arguments are not ordinary men. They are University Professors. Secondly, these Professors came out with their arguments after Prof. Gadgil had put forth the case for the inclusion of Bombay in Maharashtra. Unfortunately, no attempt has so far been made to refute the arguments of the adversaries of Prof. Gadgil. The result has been the creation of an impression that Prof. Gadgil's adversaries have carried the day. It was absolutely essential to remove this impression.

The other side

62. There are however arguments which the adversaries of Prof. Gadgil have not thought of but which may be advanced with justice as well as force in favour of the claim of Maharashtrians for the inclusion of Bombay in Maharashtra. It is quite possible that these arguments may suggest themselves to the Commission. But I don't like to leave it to chance. I therefore propose to set them out below even though the Commission might think that it was unnecessary.

Calcutta and Bombay

63. In deciding upon the issue of exclusion of Bombay from Maharashtra the Commission will have to take into account the position of Calcutta. Like Bombay it is the chief emporium of the whole of eastern part of India. Like the Maharashtrians in Bombay the Bengalis in Calcutta are in a minority. Like the Maharashtrians in Bombay, the Bengalis do not own the trade and industry of Calcutta. The position of the Bengalis vis-a-vis Calcutta is worse than the position of the Maharashtrians vis-a-vis Bombay. For, the Maharashtrians can at least claim that they have supplied labour if not capital for the trade and industry of Bombay. The Bengalis cannot even say this. If the Commission can accept the arguments urged for the separation of Bombay from Maharashtra, it must be equally prepared to recommend the separation of Calcutta from West Bengal. For it is a very pertinent question to ask that if for the reasons given Bombay can be separated from Maharashtra why when the same reasons exist Calcutta be not separated from West Bengal.

Is Bombay Viable?

64. Before Bombay can be separated it must be proved that financially Bombay is a viable Province. As I have already said if proper accounting of revenue and expenditure was made Bombay on the basis of present level of taxation may not be a self-sufficient Province. If that be so, the proposal for creating Bombay a separate Province must fall to the ground. It is no use comparing Bombay with Provinces like Orissa and Assam. The standard of administration, the standard of living and consequently the level of wages in Bombay are all sc high that I doubt that even with a crushing rate of taxation Bombay will be able to raise the necessary amount of revenue to meet the expenditure.

The aim behind Greater Bombay

65. This doubt regarding viability of Bombay Province is heightened by the indecent haste shown by the Government of Bombay in creating Greater Bombay by including within the limits of Bombay the adjoining parts of Maharashtra. It seems that the object of including such area cannot but be to make Bombay viable. What else can it be? So long as Bombay remained part of Maharashtra it did not matter to Maharashtrians In which administrative area a portion of Maharashtra was included. But when Bombay is to be a separate Province it will take a long time to make Maharashtrians part with their territory to make Bombay greater

and viable. What is more important is the scheme of greater Bombay casts responsibility upon the Linguistic Provinces Commission to decide whether they could, with justice force Maharashtrians not only to submit to the demand of the Gujarathis to give up Bombay but also to submit to their further demand to hand over a part of territory of Maharashtra to make Bombay a viable Province. The Commission cannot escape this responsibility.

66. Maharashtra and Bombay are not merely inter-dependent, they are really one and integral. Severance between the two would be fatal to both. The sources of water and electricity for Bombay lie in Maharashtra. The intelligentsia of Maharashtra lives in Bombay. To sever Bombay from Maharashtra would be to make the economic life of Bombay precarious and to dissociate the masses of Maharashtra from its intelligentsia without whose lead the masses of Maharashtra will be nowhere.

Arbitration as a Solution

67. I have seen a suggestion made in some quarters that problem of Bombay should be settled by arbitration. I have never heard of a more absurd suggestion than this. It is as absurd as the suggestion to refer matrimonial cause to arbitration, The matrimonial tie is too personal, to be severed by a third party. Bombay and Maharashtra are tied together by God to use a Biblical phrase. No arbitrator can put them asunder. The only agency which is authorized to do so is the Commission. Let it decide.

THE END